So You Want to Be a Substitute Teacher

So You Want to Be a Substitute Teacher

DR. JIMMY RICARDO HARPER

Tampa, Florida

The content associated with this book is the sole work and responsibility of the author. Gatekeeper Press had no involvement in the generation of this content.

So You Want to Be a Substitute Teacher

Published by Gatekeeper Press
7853 Gunn Hwy., Suite 209
Tampa, FL 33626
www.GatekeeperPress.com

Copyright © 2024 by Dr. Jimmy Ricardo Harper

All rights reserved. Neither this book, nor any parts within it may be sold or reproduced in any form or by any electronic or mechanical means, including information storage and retrieval systems, without permission in writing from the author. The only exception is by a reviewer, who may quote short excerpts in a review.

Library of Congress Control Number: 2024945536

ISBN (hardcover): 9781662956614
ISBN (paperback): 9781662956621
eISBN: 9781662956638

Table of Contents

Introduction   1

Chapter 1: So You Want to Be a Substitute Teacher   3

Chapter 2: What to Expect as a Substitute Teacher   7

Chapter 3: Making a Difference as a Substitute Teacher   13

Conclusion   19

Introduction

I am writing this introduction with the hope that it will inspire you to join the thousands of us in the substitute teaching profession. Being a substitute teacher is more than a job, it's a calling. When you enter the field of education as an educator/teacher, you are taking on the challenge of making a difference in the lives of students. I will be frank with you; it is rewarding but not an easy job. Students will disrespect you. They will make you so mad at times, you will say, "I don't need this." With that being said, if you want to make a difference in a young person's life, then you will stick out the bad days, because, believe me, there are *many* more good days than challenging ones. If you can handle the bad days along with the amazing ones, then you are making the right decision to become a part of the educational field.

Respect for all,

Dr. Jimmy R. Harper, DBA PhD, *substitute teacher*

CHAPTER 1

So You Want to Be a Substitute Teacher

I remember my first day as a substitute teacher. I went to the orientation session given by the district. It was a three-hour session, and there was a host of information presented.

To be honest with you, their three hours of rapid-fire information did not really prepare me for my first assignment. I started substituting at the elementary school level. That was fun. My first real assignment (where I was tested) was at a middle school in a low-income area of the school district. All of the students for the entire day were seventh graders. As the students walked into the classroom, I heard comments like "sub-sandwich; I'm not going to stay in here!" or "I'm not doing anything today." Well let me tell you, it was an interesting first day in middle school. By the end of that day, all I could say, with a smile on my face, because they pushed every button they could to get on my nerves, was "Welcome to the world of a substitute teacher." Students today come to school with a host of problems. Students have the same social problems, emotional problems, money problems, and family problems as we might have. Being a teacher, let alone a substitute teacher, you will encounter an array of personalities all at one time in an enclosed area. It does not matter where you decide to work. You will have to contend with the same attitudes from students because, regardless of location, students will be students.

A host of substitute teachers will be working in inner-city school districts, which means you will be engaging an ethnic and diverse student population. You should understand, as sad as it is, many students may not see the value of an education. That is what's going to make your job more challenging! Your job is to become their teacher for the day. As a substitute teacher, from the

Chapter 1

first bell and throughout the school day, you have to be mentally prepared to deal with students who have behavioral problems.

The biggest problem you will have to come to terms with is the lack of respect the students will give you. The ironic thing is students with behavioral problems typically don't care.

It's not that they don't know any better, it's that they just don't care. Also, and I hate to say this, but we as substitute teachers have a target painted on our backs the moment the students walk into that classroom. Taking charge of the classroom *must* be your first order of business.

Typically, teachers will leave a lesson plan, explaining what the students' assignments are for each class period of the day. Sometimes, the teacher will let you know who the troublesome students are and what type of behaviors to expect from those students. Take note, it will make your assignment easier! Teachers know their students—trust what they say.

From experience, I have learned that students will do whatever they can to do as little work as possible or nothing at all. The teacher expects you to execute the lesson plan for that day. If the teacher has been gone for a day or two, then most likely there was a substitute teacher in that classroom, and hopefully they left notes on the class behavior. I suggest that you use the previous day's notes to help guide you. Take charge, control your classroom, and get the class's attention. I let the students know what my expectations are from them. Then I explain to the students what *their* teacher expects from me; this helps me to build a rapport with them. Also, if there are students that I was told I might have issues with, I let them know, I know who they are! How you present yourself to the class will set the tone/atmosphere for acceptance and respect from the students.

To close this chapter, your takeaway should be: If the students don't respect you, they will not learn anything with you as their substitute teacher. A successful substitute teacher takes control of the classroom through establishing a rapport with the students. That's how you maintain the learning culture the teacher has established.

CHAPTER 2

What to Expect as a Substitute Teacher

As a substitute teacher, I can tell you from experience, you must employ a high degree of empathy when dealing with students. I personally enjoy walking around the classroom; it's that process of creating connections with the students. I engage the students in conversation about that day's lesson and what they think. This lets me know if they are on task or not. I ask them questions. I found that if the student feels that you understand where they are coming from, you will gain their trust. But be warned, they know when you are being genuine. The point is controlling your class is what is expected of you, but enjoying the experience and making new connections is up to you.

In classrooms today, most teachers will leave notations in their lesson plan. This information could be anything from allowing students to sit in seats other than their assigned seats or allowing students to listen to music or eating in class as long as they clean up their mess. But most of the time, they will leave it up to you to allow this treat they give the class. The point is the teacher has already established the tone/environment conducive for learning. Most importantly, the teacher expects you to maintain that environment! I have learned that establishing and reminding them of the rules is the best first step. I let the students know that I'm not there to change the dynamics of the classroom. When that is clear, I tell the students that I have three rules: (1) no talking while I'm talking; (2) no loud talking—loud talking means I don't want to hear what you are talking about if you are in the back of the classroom and my desk is all the way in front of the classroom; (3) no shouting across the room—if the student wants to talk to another student across the classroom, I normally

Chapter 2

let them go to that side of the classroom. Then I read them the teacher's notes on what the plans are for that period.

Your day will be governed by the mood via that class period. Your working environment is where most students will try to do as little as possible. The teacher is expecting you, as a substitute teacher, to get the students to do the assignment or, for the most part, be productive. When teachers leave you a note pointing out particular students and what to expect from them, use that information to create a rapport or a connection with them and the class.

Today, the chaos that is running throughout the educational system, particularly in classrooms, can most likely be traced back to social media, students' home lives, friends, groups, and the student mindset. I have learned that if behavioral problems are not corrected at the beginning, that behavior will only get worse. The point is bad behavior that is allowed to grow at an early stage of the student's educational journey will become the norm in later years. Think about it!

We as educators are working in an era where the focus for students is not on getting an education, but surviving. Students don't understand the value of an education yet. But if students just look at the area where they live and the area where their school is, you would think they would see that there is more that life has to offer. When students are able to see how getting an education can create a better environment for them, they will then understand that they can contribute positively to the world. There is a saying I like to quote that fits most of the students today: "There are none so blind as those who will not see, and the most deluded people are those who choose to ignore what they already know" (Thomas Chalkley). Expanding on that concept, the environment the student lives in has a direct correlation to their behavior in the classroom. The message we as educators must project is that their environment does not have to be an overwhelming determining factor for the outcome of their lives.

Our lives are influenced by an array of hard choices, bad choices, people, events in our lives—both positive and negative—television, radio, internet, social media, family, friends, etc. Another observation that I have made about today's students is that some have problems following rules. As a substitute teacher, you will quickly learn the difference between ninth, tenth, eleventh, and twelfth graders. You will also comprehend the learning curve for behavior in different grades really fast.

Chapter 2

For example, the freshmen, ninth graders, will tend to drive you crazy if you let them. This means they do not want to learn anything if you don't make them. The teacher that you will be subbing for will let you know what to expect from each grade level. As a substitute teacher, it is in your best interest to figure out the mindset for each grade level you will be working with.

As a substitute teacher, you will have good days and bad days; this depends on the temperament of the class. A good day is when the class does what the teacher is expecting them to do—not give the substitute any problems. A bad day is when some students want to take control of the class from you.

Some students will test you, and you should fully expect that!

Getting to know your students is critical for your success. It's hard when you are a "fly by night" substitute teacher (someone that travels from school to school all the time, with zero consistency). There is a reason why I can now distinguish between grade levels. Most of the students in higher grades (eleventh and twelfth) appear to have more self-control. The students in lower grades (ninth and tenth) appear to have very little self-control, if any at all. My opinion is, the students in the lower grades, some of them, still have the mentality of either a middle schooler or elementary schooler.

CHAPTER 3

Make a Difference as a Substitute Teacher

My experiences have led me to believe that a lot of teachers feel the same way students feel about substitute teachers. And you can't blame them! Let's be honest, most of the people that are substitute teaching today are there for a paycheck. Teachers know this and so do the students. The real question is who are you subbing for, students or the school?

Today, the substitute teaching profession is turning into big business. One thing I've noticed about some substitute teachers is they do not dress professionally. Perception is everything! Many substitute teachers come to work dressed too casually. What I mean is their attire is something less desirable. Some of them dress like they are at home on a Saturday afternoon. My point is that how you present yourself says a lot to the students and helps them form their opinion of you. Teachers will always ask students about the substitute teacher they had while they were absent. Typically, teachers listen to the students. Most importantly, the teacher will judge you by the amount of work actually done that day. If you can't follow the lesson plan, the teacher will more than likely ask that you not sub for them again. That will greatly affect your performance rating and callbacks.

Students might think of substitute teachers as overpaid babysitters. Likewise, students also think of substitute teachers as not "real" teachers. Unfortunately, a lot of substitute teachers do fall into that category. Many substitute teachers have become frustrated really fast.

Sometimes it might take a few weeks or months of handling disrespectful students.

As a substitute teacher, you will often wear more than one hat. You will become a social worker, mentor, parent, and, most importantly, an ally. Most substitute teachers sit behind the desk and play on their cell phones or the school computer. Rest assured that the students will notice that. Students are watching your every move, just as you need to be watching theirs.

We come from all walks of life. Why not use that to your advantage? Many of us are retired from a variety of professions. Some of you have not stepped into a classroom since your own high school days, let alone addressed a room full of students. It seems that a lot of substitute teachers find comfort in not truly engaging and interacting with the students. They just tell the students what to do, and that's it. They leave it up to the students to follow directions. In my opinion, that is just asking for nothing to be accomplished. However, when you engage the students in conversation, you can bring life experiences (yours or theirs) into the conversation. If you are a good listener, you will tailor your response to engage and connect with the students. Remember, there is a reason for everything. If you really want to be the type of substitute teacher that wants to truly be a positive figure, you must keep an open mind. Trust me, it is possible to make a difference! There is that old idiom, where there's a will, there's a way. You must look past the students' behavior. Remember, students are people too! You as a substitute teacher have the opportunity to be a positive force in the classroom. My mindset every day is "I have a lot to offer." I repeat this when I enter a classroom.

One day, I was talking with a school psychologist. I told her my views about students' learning. She looked at me oddly and replied, "You want to save the world, one student at a time." That stayed with me because it rang true.

You will be surprised when you see grateful students gravitate to you when they know that you really do care about how they are feeling at that moment in time. I ask them about their evening or their weekend. For example, if a student appears tired, I ask them if they had a long night. Sometimes it's the little things that catch a student's attention. In my experience, how you approach a student and the positive energy you project toward them will help you perform your job/assignment successfully and will make all the difference in the world. Whether it's one student or a classroom full of students, you have the ability to reach them all! Some students are just the way they are, and there's nothing you can do to change that, but you can still be a positive person in their lives.

Chapter 3

In closing this chapter, I will leave you with this. If you look at this job as only a paycheck, you will not make a difference to the students. It is my hope that you take this job seriously. There is plenty of work in schools for people who feel the need to get involved in the business of education—especially substitute teaching. You have the choice to be a good example of "what if" in the eyes, mind, and heart of every student you come in contact with.

Conclusion

Well, you made it to the end. If you are new or not to the world of substitute teaching, if you are new and are just curious about what to expect, I hope I've given you something to think about. The educational field has changed since I was in school. The workload is more challenging, and the pace is much quicker for students and teachers. Students, for a variety of reasons, seem to just be going through the motions of getting an education. For example, a lot of students have poor penmanship. Some students' writing is so bad that not even they can read back to you what they wrote. Frankly, you can't blame the student entirely. The educational system is just pushing students through it as fast as it can. It's frustrating for teachers when they have to cover material students should have learned one or two grades ago. It's also frustrating when students come into their classroom with poor study habits or very little comprehension/critical thinking skills. The teacher has already accepted that they are in for trouble. And then, there's you. There will be days when you will just love this job. Some reasons for this might be: the student possibly had gotten enough rest, they might have had a good meal, or they could just be in a good mood that day. I call that a good day. But when everything is going crazy and things are getting out of control in the classroom, that's the worst day for substitute teachers. One unknown is you will not know what type of day you will have until that first class of the day walks into the classroom. I know this is a lot to digest. You might be saying to yourself, "I just want to make enough money to supplement my income," which is why most people come into the world of substitute teaching. Others find that subbing is a good way to test the waters to see if they want to jump in and become a teacher. It really doesn't matter why you want to be a substitute teacher. But what does matter is that you are bringing life experiences and, hopefully, care into the profession. Be the one that leaves a positive influence behind.

In closing I want to say, you have a lot to offer the profession, the students, and the school district. The philosophies you are bringing into the classroom and the students' lives are invaluable. You, indeed, are a role model whether you want to think you are or not. You have skills that if used properly, can positively change students' lives for the better.

Conclusion

www.ingramcontent.com/pod-product-compliance
Lightning Source LLC
LaVergne TN
LVHW011901060526
838200LV00054B/4470